AF176604

MIRRAN THOUGHT

1

MIRRAN THOUGHT

Spitzwiesenstr. 50
90765 Fürth
Germany

www.dwmirran.de
www.empty.de
empty@empty.de

READ TWENTYSIX (MT-634)

Printed and published by
BoD - Books on Demand,
Norderstedt

ISBN: 978-3-7543-0338-2

First printing 2021

MIRRAN THOUGHT is the publishing arm of
Mirran Threat, a company devoted to releasing the
music and writings of the various members of Doc
Wör Mirran. Mirran Thought and Mirran Threat are
both divisions of MT Undertainment.

FSC
www.fsc.org

MIX

Papier aus ver-
antwortungsvollen
Quellen
Paper from
responsible sources

FSC® C105338

As the Ghosts
Ripped and Tore

Joseph B. Raimond

Written in Fürth Germany
2017 to 2021

As always, in loving memory of Frank
Abendroth and Tom Murphy.

For Conny, my perfect angel

Dedicated to Eric Woolfson

Cover art by Joseph B. Raimond
"As The Ghosts Ripped and Tore"
watercolor and spray-paint on paper,
Fürth Germany, 2015.

This is DWM release Nr. 185

Phonograph

No

I don't want to buy that shampoo
On sale at some shithole store
In a limited-edition bottle
And smelling of strawberries

I don't want to test drive
Your new model SUV
(stupid ugly vehicle)
With zero percent financing
If I act today!

I don't want
To enroll in your business college
And earn a bachelor in business
To get me ready for my new
Soulless, suit and tie career

I don't want to shop
In your new shopping center
With over a hundred
Brand name shops
Open till 9 pm
Only a few minutes from
The freeway exit
With lots of free parking

All I want is my record player
A cold beer and a bottle
Of good scotch
A bit of sunshine,
A warm afternoon
A pen
And a blank sheet of paper

Hate

No,
I don't hate you
I don't hate anyone
Except that fucker
Staring at me from
The mirror
That ass, that schmuck
That reminds me so much
Of his loser father

Joe Loaf

My small, unimportant
Paintings
Are like little breadcrumbs
That I drop along my journey
As I zigzag, here
Then there
Sometimes forwards
Usually backwards
To, well, somewhere
(not sure where just yet!)
The truth is
I have no clue
About where I am going

And each little
Unimportant,
Badly painted painting
If you put them all together
You would end up
With Joe Loaf
Definitely more politically correct
Than Meat Loaf
And about worth as much
As a loaf of bread

Can't Can't

Can can
Can could, and did
Splendidly

But can't
Cannot
Couldn't
Never did and won't
It just aint
In the cards

How could it ever
Have been otherwise?
When everyone claims
Allegiance, but still
Only looks out for
Number one
In fact, there isn't
And never was
A number two

So I'm left
Scratching my head
Walking alone on a lonely road
Of calling all the shots
Asking for help
And wondering
What happened
To all the promises?

**Ballerina**

I am like
A world class
Olympic gold medal
Ballerina
For all the tiptoeing I do
Around your feelings
His and her feelings
Always afraid
Of saying the wrong thing
Hurting someone's feelings
Getting on their bad side

No wonder
I am so good
At ghosting

Daddy

Once,
After one of your visits
I realized
That if I would add up
All the time
You would probably be here
With me
It would come out
To only a few weeks
In total

As if that
Was not depressing enough,
Not long after that,
You died

Suddenly

No more good German beer together
No more schnitzel dinners
No more heated political discussions
No more chances
For you to right
All the wrongs you did me

Now, nothing is left
But a few regrets
And a lot
Of unanswered questions

Thread

Your seemingly endless
Thread
Dyed in dazzling colors
Pushed and taunted
Into form and inspired color
Happily, created your art

Has now come to its end

And as we, your friends
Grasped at the end
Of your thread
In the cold, solemn hall
We thought of your life
Sang a few songs
Then went home

You, your art
One and the same
Has come to a saddened end
So suddenly

Now we must carry on
Without you
Every day, a day closer
To our own painful
And lonely end

To the ends of our own threads

Rizla

Our art stems
Like a car crash in our brains
Can be dangerous
Or life threatening
But no, let's take the safe bet
Do nothing, think nothing
Declare to the world
"I am not an artist"

But still, the craving
For attention, for praise
I will create the world's
Most collectable vinyl
Limited editions galore!
For an easy buck
And basking in my
Thieving spotlight

But oh, if I get caught
I will hate the world
Despise those wicked tongues
And burn their lawyer's letters
Those that have the gal
To protect their art
I will hate them until
My dying day
Bake in my trauma
Cry in a million-dollar house
And plan my next theft

Artistic Motives

I don't breathe
For profit
I don't breathe
For the money
I don't breathe
For fame or fortune
I don't breathe
For bubble-boobed blondes
I don't breathe
For some PhD title
I don't breathe
To hang in some museum
I don't breathe
For a best seller's list
I don't breathe
To make the top forty
I don't breathe
For a review in the New York Times
I don't breathe
For your admiration

I breathe
To stay alive

A Lifetime

All I ever wanted
Was to be timeless
If even
For just a moment

<u>Broken</u>

My America is broken
Everyone is drawing lines in the sand
Posting memes
Pulling guns

Everyone is black or white
Conservative or liberal
Republican or Democrat
Right or left
Right or wrong

Everyone is waiting
In their naïve little bubbles
For their Bernie or
Their boogaloo

And while they wait
America crumbles
America rusts
And the world moves on

As I have moved on
Turing my back on divisions
Ignorance and fear

Bye Bye Rush

Your voice was heard across the land
Sunday church, a heavy hand

Don't ask why
Don't ask why
Bye bye rush!

Your written word was wasted ink
Your box is ready, start to stink

It's time to die
For spreading lies
Bye bye rush!

I hope it hurts, I hope you're scared
No one can help, neither prayer

Don't ask why
Don't ask why
Bye bye rush!

You poison families, poison minds
But empathy you could not find

It's time to die
For spreading lies
Bye bye rush!

Silly Woman

Stomping on the face
Of mother nature
I scream at our mother
Of mothers
If I really had to be
Why couldn't I be
Exceptional?

Of A Lifetime

It took me a lifetime
To figure out what I wanted
And when I finally figured it out
It was too late
To achieve it

Civil Cold War

Intolerance, coming full circle
While lined up at the food banks
Hoarding the rotting, unwanted foodstuffs
First into our empty pickups
Then into our empty guts

Passionate in our hate
Of one another, we evil eye
Anyone that looks differently
Or, god forbid
Thinks differently
To our chosen gospel

It is only a matter of time
Before we are tired of the mean glares
And grab for our guns
But when that spark ignites
There will be no going back

The Establishment

Naïve,
Or just plain dumb?
Wading through the mud
Drenched in the sweat of endless youth
Drunk on perceived freedom
Viewing the world
Through your square shaped glasses
Teenage rebellion
As if you ruled the world
You never stood a chance
When soon enough
Gravity sagged your tits
Cholesterol clotted your veins
And stupidity conquered your mind
You became
"The establishment"
Even faster than your hated parents

The Right Expression

Use your brians, you morans
As it's not spelled socalism
Because this is America
And are only lanaguage
Is English!

We all know that your all liberials
Are really Jewish terroists
They are stealing my libety!
So, it is time to decide
Between libety and tranny

Protect our daugters!
Listen to your
Commander in theif
And give me amensty
Because we are white, proud
And have superior
Jeans

Maintenance

Sure, no problem
Sweetie
I will put down my pen
Put away my tools
Get off the ladder
Get out of the tub
Come out of the garden
Close the program
Turn off the computer

Look into your eyes
And love you

Expecting To Fly

Within the land of angels
I was engulfed
By my hell

Expecting to fly
I could barely breath
While drowning in my sorrow

And as my fellow comrades
Began to fall
I was soon left
As the last man standing

Time so cruel
Reflects my ugly image
In every mirror I avoid

The forgotten years
Pile up in a junkyard
Of mistakes and regrets

And if I have learned anything
It is that
All the promise of youth
Is but one big empty lie

All the hopes
We hold in our future
Are replaced

By the hopelessness
Of our aging
Mortal bodies

It will soon be time to go
An empty chair
Will be my legacy
Ready for the next
Sucker
Expecting to fly

Budapest

When Layla one day
Sang me her song of promise
I denied myself the joy
And again traded her love
For a life of broken promises,
Violence and indifference

But I never forgot her,
And she never gave up
And finally, one fine day
I broke free of the chains
Of sadness and longing

And although she had long moved on
I again walked that promenade
Basked in the sunshine
Of my hard-won freedom
While a band nearby
Played our song

The Ultimate Equalizer

Someday,
Far in the future
Our sun
Will supernova
And engulf our earth
In flame

Then,
It will make absolutely no difference
That I never bought that guitar
That I didn't win that Picasso painting
Or that I was pissed off
That that ass at the gas station
Short-changed me

It will absolutely no difference
That I my father was never
A member of Pink Floyd
That I never learned to play drums
Or how many people
Bought my newest album

It will make absolutely no difference
How terrible my marriage was
How much I am in love now
Or if I finally found happiness or not

It will make absolutely no difference
How high my cholesterol is

How low my blood pressure was
Or how much weight I should lose

It will make absolutely no difference
That I burned dinner yesterday
Feel depressed today
Or hope I get a raise next year

It will make absolutely no difference
How few people came to my exhibition
How much they paid for my paintings
Or that none of my works
Have so far been hung in the MOMA

It will make absolutely no difference
How many people died
In nine-eleven
Or through Trump's incompetence
In handling the Corona virus

It will make absolutely no difference
How much range
Your new electric car gets
Compared to mine
Or what color
Your new car is

It will make absolutely no difference
Who you voted for

Who you didn't vote for
Or who the vice president will be

It will make no difference
Just how terrible of a president Trump was
How many of barrels of oil were leaked today
Or how many animals have become extinct
Because of our greed

I'm feeling much better now,
Thank you

<u>Competition</u>

At my father's
Funeral
There was nobody there
Except some family
And a few drunken friends
Of my former half sister

I've got it all planned out:
At my funeral
There will be hundreds
Of both family
Cool friends
And fans
A band will play
And refreshments will be served!

I'll show you!

The Glooming Hour

Forget the naïve, midnight
"Witching hour"
That is child's play
Bedtime story fodder

The worst hour
Is usually a few hours later
When something unimportant
Like a dog barking
Somewhere far away
Slowly wakes you up

Or, you simply have to pee

And your mind starts
Like an old rusty clock
To slowly turn
And you begin to think
And contemplate
And brood

And soon enough
Every little commitment
Feels like a mountain
You must climb

Every appointment
A dreaded date of which
There is no escape

Every cent spent
Is a cent too many
And you worry
About money

It is at that dark hour
That you cry
For those lost loves

It is when it dawns on you
That all those high school
Best fiends forever
Friends
Are not ever, coming home again

It is in that gloomy hour
That you mourn
The loved ones departed, knowing now
You will never, ever
See or talk to them again

It is when you realize
That all those childish dreams
You were once so determined to fulfill
Will in the end,
Never come true
And you will never even earn
A footnote

It is when you are most convinced
That the sun
Will never rise for you again

It is when the reality
Of your own mortality
Hits you the hardest
And leaves you almost begging
For your god of choice
To go ahead
And get it over with

Honestly,

I don't care

I don't care
How many figures you earn
How much your stocks are worth
Or how little you pay in taxes

I don't care
How much your suit and tie cost
Who your tailor is
Or how good you think you look

I don't care
What cup size your wife has
Or how many silicon injected
Bubble boobed bimbos you have fucked

I don't care
When, or how, you were born again
What your god told you last night
In a dream
Or how you think I might be saved

I don't care
How many horsepower your car has
What it cost,
How fast it is
Or how it helps you to get laid

I don't care
What part of town
You can afford to live in
How much your properties are worth
Or the color of your bathroom tiles

I don't care
How much you are going to inherit
Who your are descended from
Or how smart your 1.5 children are

I don't care
What you got your
Doctor's degree in
What your grade point average was
Or how prestigious your school is

I don't care
How good you are at tennis
What your golf handicap is
Or what country club you belong to

I don't care
If you did get
Eric Clapton's autograph once
Or how many concerts
You have been to

I don't care
About your major label record deal
How big the advance was
Or how many albums you sold

I don't care
If only ten copies of some record
Were ever pressed
If the labels were misprinted
Or what color the vinyl is

I don't care
How valuable your
Butcher cover is
Or if it is in mint condition
Or not

I don't care
How big the payoff will be
When your life insurance
Pays out next year

Honestly,
I am the richest person I know
Which is why
I do not want
What I haven't got

Toom

We'd go to the toom towers
Ready for anything,
But mostly ready for a cold beer
Cool tunes and if we were (very) lucky
A few teenage breasts
Exposed and ready to fondle
By our eager, unexperienced hands

We would ignore
The honk of the school bus
On those drizzly autumn mornings
Or the walk from work
Our palms dripping blood
And the guilt
Of our crooked supervisor

We would ignore
The bodies, dropping
By our breakfast windows
Happy in death
Free from the shackles
Of a disappointing life

We would ignore
The death of Nicky's brother
His head ripped from his shoulders
In a midnight crash
Into the back of a bus
And the sobbing of his father

41

Harry would be on his drum set
Alan would be busy studying
Mike would be smoking
And I'd be dreaming

Employment

Hate
Is a hell of a lot of work

It is like a damn
Full time job
Robbing you of sleep
Sapping all your energy
It puts you in a shitty mood
Turns you into a worried
Old nag

So let the macho
Have his sports car
Let the dumb blond
Have her bubble boobs
Let the banker
Have his bonus
Let the soccer mom
Drive her SUV
Let the teenager
Have his rap
Let the politician
Have his power
Let the punker
Have his mohawk

Let all those babies
Have all their bottles

<u>Withering</u>

To my withering self
Neither savage nor exceptional
That midnight evil
Can be mighty attractive
When the light of reason
Cannot show the lines of age
Where the lines of evil
Are forever engraved in the face of death

I am the forever primitive
Always ready to climb the mountain
Of false hopes and good luck
Until the inevitable crash
The plight will take wings
And rush me tumbling
Into the dark valley of evil
Where the night is forever
And the evil in us all
Feasts on our goodwill
And love for one another

The infinity between the stars
The light years of nothing
Sings to my withering self
And in that perpetual darkness
Evil will find a home
Even in my heart

Timidity

She fondled and fumbled
Fumbled and fondled
But try as she might
The little boy
Just didn't want to come
Out to play

There was a big bad world
Trying to put its foot
Into the door
Of the small bad world
Of his childhood
And try as he might
With fantasies and hopes
His naivety won
This first important battle
And within two weeks
Their brief love
Came to an end

The Ultimate MILF

She is pretty
Doesn't show her age
Always appears young
She's got big round breasts
Spread legs
Always ready for more
Reproduction
I wanna fuck
Mother nature

Revive

Sometimes
I'm not so sure
I want to go through
All this again

Sure, I know
I always talk about it
I often dream about it
But in the end
I think I might
Back away
Turn around
And run towards
That alleged light
The eternal darkness
My final rest
And embrace
Mother nature
And decay

Uncivil War

Give me the change
Lead me away from the hate,
Away from division
I am tired,
Of the constant rage
I am tired,
Of the partition

I want rest
From the chasms of the past
The stupidity of the mob
And the ignorance of the greedy
I want a unity
Of heart and spirit
For mankind

So I can retire
And give my life
To love and art

Today is a new day
And finally, maybe I wake
With hope

Amy Apples

Daddy's ugly little
Old, stinky little dog
Finally gave up
And was soon gone
And done buried
In the far, right corner
Of the barren
Dry back yard
Under
An old apple tree

And come next summer
The tree blossomed
Like a happy little
Sapling
And presented proudly
To the world
The sweet and delicious
Amy apples

And when dad died
Part of him went under
That same old apple tree
And although
The tree didn't die
Them apples
Tasted bitter
And of regret

Wait

Sitting in the waiting room
Of my doctor
In front of me a reproduction
Of a Klee watercolor
To the left
A Sonia Delaunay

Beautiful and timeless
Works of art
Among my favorites
And I start to feel a bit less nervous

Want to cover a grand piano
In felt and grease?
Or nail a hundred plastic
Coffee cups to the wall?
Wash wooden ducks in mud?
Nail your penis to a board?
Etc………..
Go ahead,
You can even call it art if you want
But I know a pile
Of pure, grade A bullshit
When I see it
And all your art theories
Contemplations and interpretations
Won't change anything
And you wait and see,
History will prove me right

Cough

Like a pair of dirty pigs
Mating
On their way
To be butchered
I cough
To kick-start that old pump
For a few more hours
Of naïve
Bliss

Not at all
A pinball wizard
I have been known
To make a bad shot
The ball, guttered
Down the middle
Reeking of whisky and beer
I never minded,
Waiting my turn
For another shot at life
While you go whole-hog
Getting tilted and jilted
Laughing, all the way
To your Wal-mart hell

Silent Prophets

We,
The silent prophets, unseen
Know the potential beauty
Of a brush stroke
Can lose ourselves in a melody
Cry in the beauty of a poem

We,
The background warriors
Always fighting
To hold the fort of humanity
We are the stop sign
In the rat race
We live within the values
Of love

As I approach
My personal sunset
I have few regrets
For I left my mark
Found true love
And felt the brief spark
Of happiness

Soon it will be time
And I might just be ready
To move on
Into eternal silence

Son

The sun is shining
But it is still
Such a dark day

There is enough
Blue fog in my soul
To smother the world
In a blanket of gloom

Enough missed
Heartbeats
Ringing ears
Panic attacks
And couch sessions
To have the world
Whining in the gutters
Of their boring
Complacency

Citizen Joe

This land is your land
This land is my land
From the island Rügen
To the Alpen highland
From the black forest
To the Oder river
This land was made
For you and
Now,
Me

<u>Discount</u>

I'm cool,
I'm cool
See?
I've even got on my clever
Politically correct
t-shirt
So give me a medal,
Pat me on the back,
Or give me a discount

Once our concert of one is over
And the echoes of our applause fade
In our empty arenas
Then and only then
Will we see
What work will need to be done
Whose ass we will need to kick
Who gets to live, and who must die

Fist Of Laughter

As a species
We, humanity
Possess an unbearable
Arrogance over other
Earthly creatures

But
Mother nature, in her usual
Ironic and,
Ultimately,
Justified way
Created humanity
Among all species
As the only
Who can contemplate, study,
Understand and finally
Fear death

We know
What is coming

So while we spend our short
Time here on earth
Fearing our upcoming deaths
All other animals
Spend their even shorter lives
In blissful ignorance
Of their coming demise

We are the ultimate
Natural losers
The final joke of evolution

And mother nature
Sits laughing
Into her fist

International Bastard

The transient baby
Grew up here, then there
Always the new kid in class
Scowls from the boys
Giggles from the girls
The timid,
Freckle faced red-head
Nine-year-old nomad
Always on the outside,
Looking in

To lifelong friendships
And the trust of a hometown
To know every single corner
Nook and cranny, a dream

But that was not to be
As the taxi is always waiting
The train is seldom late
And the turbulent skies
Promise fear

Not anymore,
For the tired nomad
Now is forcing his love
On a new home, like it or not
Trying to catch up to the
Envied natives

Cornered

Your angry silence
Is like a concrete tomb
Enclosing me
With neither air, nor light
No sun, no music
Can penetrate
My suffocating death

The silence of your tears
As they fall
Are like the quiet
War of little insects
As the world moves on
Unaware

Cornered,
I cannot move
Without loss or pain
I can no longer fly
Through euphoria
Nor swim through your tears

All roads
Lead to
Solitude

As the Ghosts Ripped and Tore

Looking down in dismay
The spirits had no other choice
But to end this appalling folly
Of God's own image

The ugly concrete jungles
Where only the dead and dying
Feel at home
Straight line graveyards
Where the aimless bureaucrats
Blossom in their paragraphs
And pray to the rule
Of man's mighty regulation

High time to end
This rape of the word
Oh, they had their chance
They had their head-start

But giving up
In naïve arrogance
They are deemed not worthy
So the time has come
To write off the misguided
Good intentions
Give up, go home
Give this world a breather
And move on, in relief